A dedication to you,
fellow human

These mountains that you are
carrying,
you were only supposed to
climb.

Why *The Nectar of Pain?*

They asked me,
How is your soul able to
give so much love to
this world?

I said,
There is a
sweetness in
the nectar that
bees seek
for honey.

There is a
sweetness in
you that
every sting and
every pain
seek
to make love.

Do not allow your
pain to make you
bitter.
Turn it into
the sweet nectar
that your soul
contains and gives
as a sign of
strength and resilience
after
it is shattered.

The only chapter in this book:

After the end

Moving on may take stages,
yes.
But humans do not heal in
clear-cut steps,
no.
One moment,
you may feel completely healed
and the next moment,
the scent of a breeze
that reminds you of them
breathes the pain so freshly
back into your flesh
and rips your heart
into pieces
once again.
You forgive them one day,
and the next day your
self-worth
screams
into every vein of yours,
paralyzing you,
begging you
to be angry with them.

Some spend a lifetime
healing,
and some spend a lifetime
wanting to heal.

Before you start this journey,

This collection of poetry that I share from my soul with you
follows what most of us go through after experiencing a painful
heartbreak. Overall, there may be stages of healing, but
cleansing yourself of the pain day by day, hour by hour and
second by second is the real struggle. Healing is not as
predictable as we would like it to be. We may take ten steps
forward one day, and take twenty back the next day. As we
walk this journey together, some poems will address you. Some
will address the one who caused the pain. And some will
address myself. Yourself. Ourselves.

Take a deep breath.

Let's begin, after the end.

As I mourn the loss of your love,
my heart cries.
I tell the memories of you
that I love you
and that I want you back.
Your memories fight back and tell me:

He never loved you.
He never loved your smile, nor your lips.
He never loved your vision, nor your eyes.
He never loved your touch, nor the creases on your hands.
He never loved your innocence, nor your fair skin.
He never loved your thoughts, nor your mind.
He never loved your care, nor your heart.
He only loved your love and the way you loved him.
You made him king, but there was no kingdom to rule.
You put suns in his sky, but the night was his home.
You made him a knight, but there were no battles to fight.
He never loved you, but he loved
the reflection of the man he saw in your eyes.
But listen to me, my friend.
You never loved him either.
You just loved being the queen.
You loved being the sun.
You loved being the woman behind a great man.
You never loved him.
You loved having something to give.
Someone to fix. Someone to please.
You see, in love, you don't get what you want.
You get what you think you get.

Once upon a mistake,
I loved you and you loved me.

The sun shined brighter than ever in my sky,
and I felt like heaven could not be close enough
to my
happiness.

After I spilled my love into your heart,
I said to you that I was sorry for hurting you,
although I did not understand how
my love
for you
could have hurt you.

After we fought our fights
and caused each other pain,
only because I loved you and could not let you go
and you stopped loving me
and wanted me to let you go,
months upon months,
and tears upon tears,
letters inside letters,
and hopes inside hollow hopes,
I wrote to you.
I begged you
to not leave me,
but
you
left.

I wish I could
wrap my heart around you
to make you feel
how I feel about
you.

I did it again
because I was too stubborn
in my love for
you.

Like a bird with broken wings,
I stood in front of you,
and I said to you:
I cannot let you go
because I am so uninterested in a reality without you.
If I imagined falling asleep next to you
and waking up next to you,
if I imagined allowing you into my space
and allowing you to invade mine,
if I imagined growing old with you
and letting the child in me play around you,
how can I hate you?
I don't just want attention.
I want *your* attention.
I don't just want to be wanted.
I crave *you* wanting me.
I crave the love *you* had for me.
I want *you* to love me.
If it's time that you want,
I will wait.
Just tell me that we will have someday
what we had one day.

You told me that
we never had anything.
You told me
not to wait.

I often close my eyes
and replay this in my heart.

You held my hand so tightly
and took my breath away
as you softly sealed my lips with your finger.
"Slow down. Rest your soul," you said.
And with your other hand,
you shed darkness over my eyes.
With that, you stole the beats of my heart.
"I'm scared," I said.
"I know the way," you said.
We walked and walked.
We talked and talked.
You put my worries to sleep.
You ignited the warmth of love in my heart.
You became part of me.
And I was you.
We were one.
We were one.
I put my heart to sleep inside yours.
And when I opened my eyes to the sun in yours,
I saw only the sun.
Not you.
You left and stripped the heart out of me.
I am still in the forest,
lost without a map,
waiting for you to come back
and show me the way.
You said you knew the way,
remember?

I still cry every time I read this.
I still don't understand
why you left
and never came back.

Why was it so hard
for me
to let go of you?

I had no home.
And with that, I was content,
because
I never knew what it felt like
to feel like home.
So you built a home for me.
And I finally felt like I belonged.
All of my scattered pieces
suddenly
came together.
Somewhere,
I put my heart to sleep
as you cradled my worries away.
I woke up one day,
cold,
abandoned,
without a roof on top,
without windows or walls.

Without you.

And you wonder why I am unable to let you go.
Before you, I never knew what a home was.
You gave me a taste of heaven.
And with your hands, you took it away.

Once you enter heaven,
you can never live again
the same way.

Once upon a time,
like a child.
I ran to the footsteps of your door.
I left the letter I had been writing for days.
I feared you'd see me, so
I quickly knocked and hid where
I could see you but you could not see me.
For nights on end, I wrote to you with
my heart and soul.
I got lost in my lines, hoping that you'd
read me between them.
I wrote my words so they wouldn't show through my eyes.
I wrote:
"I captured the stars from the skies
and put them in your eyes.
I took the pearls from my oceans
and placed them in your hands.
I played the strings of the most beautiful melodies
to the beats of your heart.
I loved the darkness out of you.
I walked your heart home.
But I did not realize that my home became dark
and that my heart left my heart."
I waited for you to open the door,
to read my letter,
to read my heart.
As you opened the door, my heart fell.
As you opened the paper and within a moment ripped it into
pieces,
you ripped my heart out again,
as you did
once upon a time.

Now I realize that
you cannot make someone
listen to you or hear you
if they do not want to.

One day,
you will tell me that
you wish you never left.
And I will tell you that
I wish you never came back,
that I wish that you did not walk away.
But you did walk away.
You will tell me that you missed
the look of love in my eyes.
And I will ask you if you missed
the tears that my eyes cried
the day that you walked away.
You will tell me that you wish
I would give you another chance.
And I will tell you that I wished
you never walked away
when you walked away.
But you still walked away.
You will tell me that you were not
yourself when you walked away.
And I will tell you that I was not
myself when I thought that
you were the one.
So do me a favour and walk away,
this time because I do not
want you to stay.

Now I know that it's important
to realize the power I have
over your presence in my life.
Even though you chose to walk away,
it doesn't mean that I was abandoned.
I could choose to walk the other way, too.

You told me that you were broken
and that you wanted to heal.
I did not know that your soul was glass.
I did not know that your heart was dark.
You aimed the broken pieces of your soul at my heart like
arrows.
I broke my soul trying to mend yours.
My fingertips bled as I
weaved your soul back together.
And my eyes dried up from the tears of my pain.
I always believed that pain cleanses your soul as rain cleanses
the
earth.
So I let my heart storm through my eyes.
And once your soul came back together,
you told me that
I
was broken.
You told me that you were not a doctor
and that your words were just words.
You told me to move out of your way,
because who would want a wounded soul like mine?
And now I turn to my heart.
I turn to myself to say:
My dear heart,
forgive me.
Forgive me for breaking you as I healed others.
Forgive me for making you beat to the happiness of others.
Forgive me
for not listening to you.
I promise you from today,
I promise you from this moment,
to put you first.
And put me first.

Now I realize
the power of
forgiving myself.

There once was a spark for you
that built a home in my eyes.
And with every step you took
further away from me,
the night sky fell into my eyes.
It turns out that not every song is worth
singing,
not every mountain is worth
climbing,
not every race is worth
running,
and not every war is worth
fighting.

I loved the parts of you that I did not
own.
And you owned the parts of me that you did not
love.

So I am taking my love back
today.
And today, I am giving
yourself
back to you.

Just because you choose not to
climb a mountain,
it does not mean that you have to
carry it.

Everyone who tells you that they know how love works
tells you what did not work with them.
Just because it did not work for them,
it does not mean that it will not work for you.
Some fall in love in moments,
and some fall after days.

Some fall in love over the years,
and some spend years
falling
in love.
Some realize after years that it was not
love.
Some fall in love with their eyes.
Some fall in love with what they hear.
Some fall in love with the feeling of
falling
in love.
Some express their love with words.
Some express their love with action.
Some express their love through touch.
And some need touch to feel love.

Some need flowers to feel loved.
Some need diamonds to feel loved.
Some need words, and some need promises.

In love,
you get what you accept.
In love,
you get what giving
gives your soul.

*I've learned not to listen to what
doesn't work,
but to what does work.*

I look back at the moment
I knew that I fell in love
with you.
I wanted to tell the world
what it felt like,
so I wrote:

I never knew what they meant when they said, "you'll know,"
until
I knew.
And I never knew what they meant when they said, "time
heals,"
until
I felt free.

Now I know
that I never really knew
and that I am free
not because I left you,
but because I came back to
myself.

To you,
reading this,
I will not tell you that
"you'll know" or
that "time will heal"
because, to you, my words might sound like
they once sounded to me,
but

I will tell you that
I would not trade all of the waiting
and all of the pain
for the beauty that these two moments
spilled in my heart
when I felt them.
You will feel like
your heart
was lifted
from the depth of this
heavy ocean,
and on your wings
that you thought were broken,
your heart will fly and,
in a new sky,
build a home.

I ran to the moon
and knelt to the ground.
Out of breath, I gasped.
I cried
and cried and cried.

You told me that just like you shined in the night,
my hope should shine in my sky.
I listened to you.
So I loved.
And my heart was broken.
I trusted.
And my trust was betrayed.
I befriended.
And my secrets were exposed.
I gave.
And I was punished for giving.
I dreamt.
And the night fell into my dreams.
So tell me.
Do I swear off love?
Do I keep my lips sealed and bury my secrets in silence?
Do I lock the treasures in my heart and build walls around
them?
And do I dream my dreams out of my soul?
Tell me.
Do I hate whom I loved?
And betray their trust as they did mine?
Do I tell their secrets as they told mine?
And do I start taking more than I give?
Do I tell my dreams to stop singing me to sleep?
Tell me.

The moon looked at me and said:
"The clouds conceal me every night.
Does that make me stop believing that there is
an earth beyond them?"

Asking me to understand why
you no longer love me
is like asking me to understand why
I am no longer worthy of being loved.
I am confident, and
my self-esteem is resilient, but
asking a soul to accept that
the love it once had
is no longer there
is like
telling a bird that
the sky
that it's used to flying in
no longer wants it to fly.

Every bird loves to fly
in its sky, and
every soul loves
to be loved
by the one that it loves.

You promised not to walk away
so I built a home for you
inside my heart.
Your voice,
your promises and
your laugh
filled it with life
and love.
And now all I hear when I enter is
the echo of
your anger and
your deafening silence
that I never deserved.
So I fall to my knees and
I crumble in the corner where
I once dreamt you'd hold me.
And I choke on the dust of the
butterflies
that fell from my stomach for you
and the tears that
hailed
from my eyes for you.

When I was struggling with letting you
go,
I wish someone had told me:

I know that you're struggling,
and I know that it's hard.
Believe me when I tell you that
I know why you put up that guard.
Perhaps they ignore you.
Perhaps they don't care.

Perhaps they won't tell you
how it is that they feel.

Perhaps they abandoned you,
or little by little are letting go of you.

Perhaps you even have no one
to relate this poem to.
I can't tell you that it will get better,
because that's probably what they all say.
What I can tell you is that I understand you
and I think that you deserve better.
Don't force yourself into places where
you don't belong.
Don't force yourself to believe what
you know is not true.
I know that you're struggling,
and I know that it's hard.

I promise to stand by you
and help you take down
that guard.

You were my home
for so long.
Now I realize that humans
cannot
be homes.
If homes can leave,
then they are not
homes.
Homes stay,
but you walked
away.

A weakness within me has shattered the walls I've built within
myself, against myself.

I may have been successful at giving,
but I never know when to stop.

I worked so hard to break down others' walls that
I forgot to break down my own.

I worked so hard to understand others' silence,
but I forgot to understand my own.

I lifted, with every bit of me,
the weight off of so many people's shoulders and hearts, but
I forgot about my own burdens.

My bones have been bruised by the burdens I've accumulated.

My heart has been beating slower and slower.

My thoughts cannot bear the chaos in my mind.

So I decided to surrender.

I give up.

And if I were to hide my wings and bundle myself
back up into my cocoon, would you then try to take what I
give,
understand my silence, or lift the weight off my shoulders?

Feeling like you will give up
does not mean that you
have to
give up.

To a Narcissist Who Moved On

I hope she knows better
and gets out of your venomous
throat
before you poison her
soul
like you poisoned mine.
I hope she has the strength
to deal with you
leaving
after you strip
the life out of her body,
the color out of her eyes,
and the love out of her heart.
I hope she does not define her self-worth
through your eyes that see
women as objects to satisfy
the lust of your hollow soul.

It irritates me to write such
strong and heartless
words, but
I've seen pain
that led a fire to ignite
in my veins.

Take your memories with all your pain.
Take it all.
I want to be free.
It was not your love that you chained me with,
but your wanting of me.
I used to think that happiness was not possible
before I see you regretting
walking away from me.

But now I know that if a man like you
had the heart to walk away from a woman like me,
what is the use of having you regret
leaving me?

I have been dwelling in a dark place,
thinking that if
you
left me,
then something must be wrong
with me.

The day we decided it's best to part ways:

My tears silently streamed
down my face.
You raised your hand
to wipe my tears but
put it back down when
you realized that could
hurt us both.
You told me:
"I don't want you to be sad."
I looked at you when
I did not want to and
I told you:
"There will always be
sadness
when it comes to you
because
you will always be the one
I want to be with
but
fate will never
destine that for us."

I do not hate you,
but I hate that I allowed
your hate
to make me
hate me.

Even if you came begging for me,
I do not want your love
because
I finally learned
that I don't need you
to love
me.

Just because I loved you,
and just because you hurt me,
I will not be ashamed to say that I loved you.
Because I really did love you.
I loved the loving person that
you were.
I do not love the cold person that you are now.
I loved the considerate person that
you were.
I do not love the inconsiderate person that you are now.
I loved the thoughtful person that
you were.
I do not love the deaf-hearted person that you are now.
You see, you once asked me what I loved about you.
And that is what I loved.
If you ask me today what I love about you,
I will tell you this:

I love the memory of the person that you
used to be.
I love that you allowed me to feel
the love that my heart can
contain.

I love the love that you showed me I can give.
I love the happiness that you showed me I could feel.
I love that you walked away.
I love that you did not stay.
I would have suffered if you stayed,
because of the person that you are
today.

I asked you what I meant to you,
with my heart beating out of my chest.

I was afraid of losing you
if you did not pass this test.

I told you that I was tired
of reading between the lines.

I asked you to tell me
if you could see the spark in my eyes.

I told you that I was ready to walk away
and never speak to you after this day.

If you could just tell me
if *you* wanted *me* to stay.

You asked me what I wanted,
your honesty, confidence, loyalty, or perhaps more?

I told you that I wanted it all,
with some love and a spark in your eyes that I'd
forever
adore.

I told you that I wanted you
to try harder.

You promised me to do so,
but, oh, how I wish I was smarter.

Now I realize that when you ask for love,
it's not as true as when it comes your way.
And when the lines are blurred,
your search for love may have gone too far
astray.

Do You Know?

-Part 1-

Do you know what it feels like to be put on a race track
and told to run
and run and run
with no end in sight?

Do you know what it feels like to continue on a road
that you know has no destination,
just because you are afraid of not having any other road
if you left the one that you're on?

Do you know what it feels like to be forced to jump
off a cliff
knowing that you have no wings
to lift you?

Do you know what it feels like to shout
and scream
and yell
your heart out,
knowing that everyone is listening
but pretending not to hear?

I do.

-Part 2-

Do you know what it feels like to believe
that you are a mistake
and that feeling pain
means that you have no control of your feelings?

Do you know what it feels like to be given the shovel
to dig deeper and deeper
only to find out when it's too late
that it's for yourself
and that there's no one waiting
to lift you out of the hole?

Do you know what it feels like to fight a battle
with no possible pain inflicted upon anyone
but yourself?

Do you know what it feels like to be wounded
and told that you caused the
wound to yourself by choosing to be where
the harm landed?

Do you know what choking on
injustice
feels like?
Do you know what it feels like to know that silence
is your best choice
when your words can no longer
be held inside of you as a
hostage?

I hope you never know that feeling,
because that is how you made me feel.
And I would never wish this kind of
pain
upon anyone.

Darling.

There are those who will light up your sky
and those whose sky you will light up.

There are those who will love you for who you are
and those who you will crave being yourself around.

There are those who will dive into your ocean
and those whose depth you will want to drown in.

There are those who will make your heart flutter with
happiness
and those whose hearts will flutter at your sight.

There are those whom you will love
and those who will love you.

And if the ones you love
love you back,
darling, you will forever see joy.

But if they feel the same way you feel about them towards
someone else,
darling, that will be a disaster.

You may be a disaster for a day,
a month,
or a year.

Just don't be a disaster forever.

Find the harbor of safety.
And find the one who feels about you
the same way you feel about them.

I wrote this to myself and
to every broken soul
out there.

To my first love.

One day, you will ask for my forgiveness.
And I will tell you this.

Where were your sweet words when your lies tainted my soul?
Where was your loyalty when your broken promises broke my
heart?

Where were your tears when my eyes choked on mine?
Where was your heart when my beats fainted in my chest?

Where was your pain when mine ran through my veins?
Where was your love when mine for you lit through my eyes?

Where was your light when you captured the moon from my
night?
Where was your depth when you took the pearls from my
ocean?

Can you remove the darkness that you shed from my soul?
Can you mend the promises that you broke?

Can you cry my tears back into smiles?
Can you beat the beats back into my heart?

Can you cleanse the pain from my veins?
Or can you weave my love for you back into my eyes?

Can you put the moon back into my night?
Can I trust you with an ocean
that you've already stolen?

If it's my forgiveness that you want,
take it.

It is not for you,
but for me.

Take it and walk away,
but don't you wait for more.

The doors you closed have been welded shut.
And the keys have been thrown into the seventh sky.

You are weak. So weak.
Take my hand. Let me help you.
Please.
You build your self-esteem by breaking others'.
You love yourself by hating on others.
You raise yourself by stepping on others.
You build your empire by sending your arrows
into the hearts of others.
You occupy their peaceful homes and claim them to be yours.
You are weak. So weak.
Because, without others, your home is empty.
Spit your venom.
And listen to me.
Take your arrows out of my heart.
Take your misery out of my home.
Watch me fly on the wings of the pain you caused me.
Watch me soar with the voice you thought I never had.
Watch me love with the heart you claimed I didn't have.
Wait.
Don't watch me.
Just get out of my way.
And let me be.

For so long,
you made me feel
that I was weak.
It is you who was weak
for not feeling.
I was the hero
for feeling.

Your love flies my soul to the moon.
It makes the sun revolve around my heart
and the stars dance in my eyes.

Your tenderness throws me in the ocean.
It plants pearls in my heart
and lifts me to the sky.

Your touch sends butterflies down my veins.
It makes roses grow in my heart
and sews my pains into traces of smoke.

Your strength cradles my heart to sleep.
It beats my heart to life
and breathes my soul to paradise.

I once felt this way
about you.

I once wrote you:
I don't care if
the whole world
looks in a direction
opposite from mine.
If you look at me,
the whole world is mine.

*I should have written that to
myself.*

Streets

If you knew how many streets I avoid
to avoid you
and memories of you,
you would leave your streets
and your cities.
If the streets I avoided to avoid you
and memories of you
knew,
they would change their names
so you
could find other streets
to put your footsteps on.

If only you knew.

I wonder at what point
love escaped us and
we
became
you
and
I.
I wonder when
love decided
to escape from our souls.
Or did our souls
let go
of love?

Prisons

We had a moment
once
when I felt that
we
were
one,
in the same feeling,
in the same soul.
But I've come to learn
that these moments
can imprison us for
years
when they were only
moments
followed by many more
that were not
the same.

I am tired of looking
out the same window,
remembering the moments
I was happy when
I looked out,
because
now all I feel is
sadness over
that happiness
no longer being there.

Rainy days
and rainy windows
imprint moments on
our hearts.

The moments that you choose to be
silent
when someone's soul is
screaming at you,
begging you to say,
"My heart is with you,"
those moments leave
scars on our souls
that no amount of excuses can
erase.
If you love someone,
you love them.
You don't allow your pride to
stop you from expressing your love
to them.
If you expect them to understand
your love through silence,
don't be surprised when their soul
slips out of your hands in silence.

It's painful,
you know,
to not know what you mean anymore
to the one whose love was louder than
thunder
at first.

You changed.
And that is painful.

The day I fell
for you:

"I don't feel ready,"
I said.
"We're never ready,"
you replied.

Now I know that
you were talking about
life,
not just us.

Opening Up

"I'm sorry if
I stirred up unwanted
memories,"
I said.
After moments of silence,
you said:
"Stirring is good."

I wish I had never attempted
to stir the chaos in
your soul.
The tornado within you
took me
with it
by accident.

2:37 a.m.

"Are you awake?"
"Yes."
"I can't sleep."
"You should try.
Sweet dreams."

That was you drawing me in
and me
resisting
falling for you.
You knew it was wrong.
I wish you had done what was right.

You told me once,
"You are a good woman."
Thank you.
You don't have to say that.
"I don't say it because
I have to.
I say it because
I want to."

I wish you never
wanted to.

The day that uncertainty
finally ended my patience with you,
I said:

"I am so tired of
not knowing
what I am to you.
So I decided to
walk away and
send my love to you
through thoughts
and prayers."
You said,
"Take a step back.
You're overthinking again.
Take a deep breath."

I look back, and I wish
I told you,
I am not
your patient.

If you ever come back,
I will tell you:

The sun is
closer to you
than I will
ever be.
So burn,
if you wish.
You will not
see the shadow of
me
even if you
become
the sun
yourself.

I am not arrogant,
but you left a scar on my heart
that turns blue
every time I think of
you.

For every time you ignored me:

You make me
wait for you to
decide
that talking to me
is what you need.
You make me feel like
what I have to say is not important.
You silence me
through your silence.
You cage my heart
through your selfishness,
and when I ask you why
you're so quiet,
you tell me that
I am being selfish.

Forgive me, your highness,
for taking away from your time.
If you truly cared,
you would apologize for ignoring me,
rather than
bury me
deeper into the ground.

When I started feeling that
you wanted to walk away:

My heart tells me
that your heart has
abandoned
the idea of
us.
You struggle to tell me that
you no longer want me
because you know,
you know,
that you will hurt me.
So you avoid saying
what needs to be said.
You chain me every once in a while
with a charming word or two.
You give me just enough
hope
to keep me holding on.

What a coward you are
to not be able to face your
own
truth.

Every time I confronted you for doing
what does not honor
the meaning of
us:

They say that time heals.
And you thought that meant
if you ignored what I said
for a while,
that I would forget it,
that I would come crawling to you,
begging you,
pleading my case,
asking you to forget
what I said.
You thought I would
remind you that my words
came out of love for you,
not wanting to punish you.

No, sir,
no.
If my words are not worth your time,
go find someone else to
care about you.
If my words mean
nothing
to you,
go find someone whose words mean
something
to you.

We both know the end has come,
but
you do not want to tell me that
because you know that
I am a good woman,
as you told me many times.
To you,
it is much easier
to not say a word.
To me,
I choke on my words
if I do not say them.

What truly hurts me
is that you know
that your silence
infects a storm in my mind,
yet you choose it
oh so
easily.

Fate Once Told Me

-Part 1-

And after all this time,
fate whispered in my ear and said:
Slow down. Rest your heart.
In my hands, you are not only human.
You are much more.
Some days you will be tested.
Some days you will be the test.
Prepare to be failed.
Some days you will be the archer.
Some days you will be the goal.
Prepare to be hurt.
Some days you will open and close doors.
Some days you will be the key.
Prepare to be used and left behind.
Some days you will be the leader.
Some days you will be a follower.
Prepare to reach a destination other than your own.
Some days you will be inspired.
Some days you will be an inspiration.
Prepare to be just an idea.
You are destined to lose and be lost.
You are destined to walk some people home.
You are destined to wander.
You are destined to see perfection.
You are destined to be flawed.
But if you befriend me, I shall tell you the secret that will free
your heart of its concerns.

-Part 2-

Worry not about the future.
You might not go there.
Live not in the past.
Its doors are locked.
Its keys are in the skies.
But remember this:
Your heart is a castle.
Guard it with a cage of gold.
Only he who is destined to enter it will seek the key.
Your mind is a kingdom of grace.
Keep its gates high and mighty.
Keep it guarded with your faith.
Befriend silence.
It never betrays you.
You are the master of your journey.
You are the owner of your path.
You are a bird, but unless you fly, you are not free.
But only after your wings are broken will you realize
that freedom is in your hands.
So be free.

I read this to you
once
and you had nothing to say.
Perhaps it's because you knew
that you were not the one
destined
to enter my heart.

The difference between
you needing
space for a while
and
you needing space forever is
space makes me miss you
but an end makes me hate you
for leaving when you promised
you'd stay.

Please don't make me
grieve you
while you're still alive.

To you,
I hope that your soul
meets its fate
at the most beautiful,
pure
and spontaneous
moment.

To those who think that love is a game:

I don't play games.
And I don't play hard to get.
I don't keep you in suspense
or fear that I will leave
out of the blue.
I don't say what I don't mean
just to charm you.
And I don't keep you waiting
just so you can think that I'm too busy
for you
or that I'm not always thinking of you.
Because, if I love you,
and want to spend the rest of my life with you,
I don't want to make you chase me.
I'm tired of running.
If I love you, you will take
a front row seat
in my mind,
because I respect your presence in my life
as my companion
and father of my children.
You will be my number-one priority,
not because I'm weak
or because I'm dependent on your love,
but because I'm a woman,
not a girl.

Love is safe.
Love is vulnerable.
If you want someone who will make you run after her love,
find her elsewhere.
That never was
and never will be
me.

I am going back again to
memories of you.
It makes me stronger
when I see how far
I've come
from you.

We sat in the office of the judge,
the one who was meant to help us
end in peace.

I told you that
if you told me that
you truly cared about me,
and that you decided to walk away
for reasons other than
who I am,
that I would forgive you.
You looked down at your
fingertips,
looked back up,
and said:
"I did not know
that your love for me
was this deep."

That is when I knew
that you meant everything that you
ever said,
but
you did not know the depth of
your own words.

My soul is aching for me
to come back to
myself.

When my soul
aches
to the point of crushing,
the only medicine
I need
are the arms of
my mother.

I look back to the day
that I told you for the
millionth
time that I felt that
you were distant.

You could have said:
"I am with you,"
but you said:
"Please.
Stop.
Obsessing."

At that time,
I did not know that
your unwillingness to comfort me
was a sign that I needed to
walk away.

To the past me.
To my future daughter.
To you:

Don't fall in love with the
first person who
tells you that they love you.
It could be that they fell in love
with the shape of your hips
or the colors of your eyes,
the scent of your skin
or the journeys that
the sight of your lips
takes them on.
They might not be seeing what you've been
needing
to be seen about you.
They might not be hearing
the voice
that you've been
needing
to be heard.
Just because they're looking,
it does not mean that they're
truly seeing.
Just because they're listening,
it does not mean that they're
truly understanding.

I wish I knew this back then,
but how would I know
this
if it did not
happen to me?

You tried to tell me that
the reason I loved you was
that I had issues with my father's
love for me.

It's a shame for you
to belittle my love for you
like that,
to say that I loved you
to compensate for the love
that I did not get from my
father.
I love my father more than oceans
love the reflection of the sky
in them.
My father's love for me
has broken the oceans to
raise me into the woman that
I am.

The love of no man
could fulfil the love
that you need to give yourself.
What about those who grew up with
no father?
Are they incomplete?
Please don't blame
anyone's lack of love for you
for loving the wrong person.

It is better to wait years
for the right love
than to stay in love
with someone who does not
love you
just so you can say that you are
in love.

You cannot be anyone's
savior:

When you were carrying too many
mountains
on your shoulders,
I told you, "your voice said more than
your words
said."
Your voice struck thunder in my heart
more than your words
explained why you were so down.
You told me:
"I thought I was talking."

You really did not talk.
You just wanted me to feel guilty for
you
feeling down,
to continue
asking you what was
weighing so heavily on your heart,
so I could figure out
and offer to give you
what you needed
without you asking for it.

The day you confessed your love:

I waited to see you
outside.
And with my heart beating outside
my chest,
I said:
"Can we talk?"
"Of course," you said.

I still cannot
finish this poem,
because every time I think back
to that day,
I feel like you stabbed my soul
over and over
by telling me that you loved me
when you
truly
did not love me.

I fell in love with you
the day you showed me your
soul.
And I spent days,
months,
and a year and
part of a year
realizing that you covered
your soul again
because you could not handle
the love
that I was touching you
with.

I spent more time getting
over you
than I spent
falling in love with you.

If I could turn back
words
and speak to you in
time,
you would know that my love is
timeless
and that years have no power to
restrain
the love that my heart
can give.

You allowed the years to
sentence
your heart to a lifetime of
no true,
deep,
and selfless
love.

The thought of you coming back
scares the butterflies in my stomach.
It makes them escape through
my soul.
You see,
I loved the person that you once
were,
not the person that you are today.
I know that if you come back,
my heart will feel
guilty
for not giving you a chance
at revealing your soul again.
But
I know that I will feel
forced
to let you back in, as
you forced me to
let go of
you.

I hope that you don't come back,
but if you do,
I will tell you this:
When you let go of me,
I felt that I could not
heal
unless you came back.
Your resistance taught me
one of the best lessons
that I ever learned.

It is not our
need
for someone that
heals us,
nor is it our
want
for them.
No person can heal us.
Only
love
can.
And the same power that created
humans with hearts
can create love too.

You were such a mountain
when I wanted to get back into
your life.
Thank you for forcing me to
climb the heartache that you put me through
instead of giving it back to me
again.

I used the bricks that you
placed on my heart to
build a home for the
love
within me.
I filled it with love for
sincerity,
kindness,
and honesty.
So I will force you out,
and I hope that you will learn the same
lessons
that I learned.
I hope that you build the same home
in your soul that I built
in mine.
I will help you
just as you helped me:
by leaving the door of my heart
closed
to you.

I am not cold,
nor am I holding a grudge against you.
I don't believe in giving people a taste of their
own medicine.
But
perhaps your broken soul
that is hanging by a thread
needs to shatter while
knocking on my door
so that it can heal.

I don't hate you.
I simply think it's impossible to
hate someone you
once truly loved.
But I often find myself wondering
why you awakened within me the
feelings that you were not
willing to continue
taking care of.
I never asked you to walk into
my life.

Many times, at
red lights,
I ache.

What hurts more than
anything
when I think back to it all
is how you say that it was all
in my head.
"I never laid a hand on you,"
you say.
"You talk as if we've been
one
for a
decade,"
you repeat.
Over and over.
Let me tell you,
sir,
that love that touches the
soul
for one moment
transcends the mysteries of
love that touches the
body
for decades.

Now that I know
what I know,
I am so thankful
for not allowing your body to
touch mine
before I knew that your soul
truly loved mine.

It is our
story
that haunts me,
not wanting you back
into my life.

It is not you that I
cannot get over.

It is the pain and
the wounds that keep
bleeding every time I think of you
or hear your name.
It is the scars that I have to hide
everywhere I go
that I cannot get over.

When I think of you,
I don't see your face anymore.
I see a shadow.
I see pain.
Yes, I
see
pain.

I often come back to
the memories of you
and the pain of you,
not because I want to
be in pain,
not because I don't want to
move on,
but because they are a
home
that welcomes me
more than my
reality
does.

When you find comfort in
sadness,
it means that you need to
feel it
and walk it
gently
out of your
soul.

I used to say that
I lost you.
Then I said that
you lost me.

*Now I say that
you were not meant for
me and
I was not meant for
you.
Thank destiny for
parting our ways
before one of our souls
bled to
death.*

Don't tell me that
words
mean nothing with no
action.
You only say it when it is
convenient for
you.

We have betrayed our
words by saying that
promises mean
nothing.

I have scars on my bones from
broken promises.

You came to me with
broken wings.
I helped you heal your
wounds
by pouring love into the
broken pieces of
your soul.
You flew away
when your wings were healed.
You left me here,
chained to the ground,
trying to remove the shards
that got stuck in my own wings
as I took them out of yours.

Where did gratefulness
go?
I will not let your deception
make me not help more
broken wings out there.
Your lack of gratitude
will not make me
not give.
I do not give just to
be thanked.
But it does not mean that
it does not hurt.

It hurts me that
someone like you
hurt a kind soul like mine
and turned around to say
that something was wrong
with me.
I console myself by
reminding myself that
while I am sitting here
wondering what is wrong with
me,
you
are the one who is
broken.
You are the one who needs
fixing,
not me.
Your wings may have healed
enough to allow you to fly,
but your soul has not
healed if it has not learned
to give.

Your heart walked away
before you did.

I must have
overdosed on
the idea
of
you.

I loved you the
right
kind of love, but
time
was not on my side.

I learned to differentiate between
loving the right
way
and loving the right
person.

When a new opportunity for love
comes your way,
do not judge it based on
what your last partner had that
the new one
does not have.
Do not base it on how thankful
you are that the new one
does not have the same
flaws
that the old one had that
you hated.
Base it not on how much better the
new person is.
Base it on who they are.
Base it on whether their journey
fits with
yours.

You will keep getting
let down and
let go
by them
until you realize the importance of
you holding your soul together,
until you realize the importance of you
keeping yourself lifted up.
You.
Yourself.
Without anyone.

I wish you knew
how much beauty is within
your soul.
You do not
need
anyone to love you to
feel
that you are worthy
of being loved.

You love those who don't love you,
to the point of giving them your soul
if they needed it.
But you cannot love your own soul to
make sure that it is stitched together?
Isn't the love that you give them
a reflection of the love
that your soul contains?
So, if they don't want that love,
why don't you give it
back
to yourself?

You become empty when
all you do is give
without giving
your own
self.

*The one who deserves you will
tell you:*

Tell me your fears, and I will
fight them
with you.
Your fears are not bigger than
us.
I have fears, too.
Let's walk through our fears
together
to get to the safety
that
our souls
long for.

Thank you for silencing me.
You led me to break
the silence of thousands who
have met humans like you
who chose not to use their hearts to love,
to allow their consciences to be just
or their broken pasts to heal
the wounds of the broken.
Thank you for loving me only when
you needed someone to love you.
You led me to understand
that in times of our need for love,
our hearts are the most beautiful.
Thank you for leaving me when
I needed you most.
You led me to myself.
You led me to needing my own heart.
You led me to my voice.

Don't you ever think that
I will hate you.
You taught me more than
any book
could ever teach me about
love,
life,
and authenticity with my feelings.

How many
times
do we have to end this
before
we really
end
it?

Stop trying to bang
feeling out of their silence.

I knew that I fell
from your heart
the night that
sleep
fell from my
eyes
because of your pain.

I am tired of looking for
reasons.

I know that I am a good person.
How could
I
be the reason
for this end?

I told you that I was in pain,
and when you asked me why,
I told you that you took so much from me.
I gave you
love.
I gave you
time.
I believed in you.
But you turned out to be
the biggest disappointment
of my life.
You asked me what you owed me,
and I told you,
"Nothing that you could give me back."

Some scars are
seared
on our souls
for eternity to
witness.

My heart aches in
corners
I did not know
existed.

Flashback.

"You love too hard,"
he said.
"It's the only way to love,"
I replied.

I am tired of
every person coming my way
telling me that I am too
needy for love.
I am not needy
for love.
I just love.

After you said your goodbye:

One day,
I will look back to you.
You will either be the best thing
that ever happened to me
or the worst mistake I ever made.
But what I know for now is this:
you leaving hurts like death,
but I owe it to myself to
not hold on
to what let go of me.
So, today, my love,
I say my goodbye to you,
too.

How many times will I say this before
I stop thinking back to you?

Don't quickly tell your
new love
about your first one.
Let not your new relationship
be based on a
broken one.
Talk about the life that you both
want,
not the life that you had.
Talk about your pains,
not your wounds.

And if you have scars,
let your scars speak
their stories
on their own.

If you choose not to
listen to this advice,
that is okay, too.
Just be aware of the
reasons
that you share what you
choose
to share.

For your new love:

When two sad souls
meet,
silence
of the lips becomes
so beautiful
as both souls
dance in
understanding.

Allow your eyes to speak
a story that
words cannot explain.
Allow your smile to sing
a beautiful melody
to the beats of your heart.
Allow your heart to beat to
the rhythm of a happiness
untold.
Allow your mind to sail
a thousand ships to the shore
of serenity.
Be brave.
Be happy.

Don't seek love
just to be in love.

Better wait years for the
right person
than wait years
for the right love
from the
wrong person.

If they don't fall in love
with your mind,
their love for you
will not overcome
the storms.

If it was my
heart that you loved
and my mind that you
valued,
you would have never
let go
of my hand.

After I finally accepted your goodbye:

I told you how much
I loved you and how much you
loving me
meant to me.
I told you that if
I looked at my whole life,
you were one of the best things
that happened to me.
I asked you to forgive me
for all of the hurtful words that
I said.
I only said them because
I was so angry that
you stopped loving me.
So you said: "Okay."
And I said:
"This is exactly why we are here.
I deal with my feelings by
expressing them, and
you deal with yours by
avoiding them."
We both went silent.
You, because you knew I was saying
the truth,
and me, because I knew
there was nothing left to say.

I drowned in your
sky,
but you flew over
my ocean.

You were never deep,
but I was brave enough
to fly
when my wings were
still young.

I once wrote:

I fear one day that
you will
forget me like I
forgot
myself the day
I loved you.
If you forget me,
and I forget me,
who will remember
myself back to
me?

Now I know that
loving someone does not mean
losing yourself.
Instead, it means
finding yourself.

Un-lose yourself.

I choke on words
that I want to say to
you,
questions that
I want to ask
you.
But I would rather keep them
inside of me and hurt than
blame you for
me
choosing to believe
everything you said.
Maybe you meant it all but
you just don't feel it
anymore.
I can't be angry with fate for not
destining you for me, so
I will let my words choke on
my tears because I can't keep trying
to find what's no longer
there.

I take the longest routes
to avoid the places that
remind me
of you:
the place you told me that
you loved me,
the place I told
you
that I loved
you.

The places that remind me of you
remind me of
everything that
I wanted to be
to you
and everything that
I am not
to you.

Wanted.
Am not.

Breathe love
into the broken
pieces of their
soul.

When each piece is
loved on its own,
they gravitate towards
one another to become
whole
again.

Put your soul back
together
first.

Carry my heart
with your soul.
I beg you.
Rock my fears to sleep.
Love my soul
back to life.

Why was I asking you
to do what
I needed to do
myself?

If you gave them
once
the love that they did not
deserve,
they will come back for more.
They will deny that they ever
caused you pain.
They will deny that they ever
poisoned your soul,
and they will come back
asking for more.
You gave it once.
They know that you will
give it
again.

Why do you fixate
so much on what they
might do?
To heal,
you should focus on what
you
do.
Not them.

They do everything to
dim
your light,
and then they ask you why
you're not shining.

Broken wings are a sign of
struggle.
And strength.

If I could turn back time,
you would still lie to me, and
I would still believe you.
I am made of unconditional belief in
goodness, and you decided to
put your goodness to sleep.
What I believe in defines me,
not what you say about me.
And what you believe in defines you,
not what you say about yourself.

I can't tell you how to love me, but
I can tell you this.
I don't want wrapped
gifts or
wrapped words.
I want
sincerity and
honesty.
If it doesn't feel like
love, don't
do it. Don't
say it.

You asked me what I wanted
from you.
So I told you.

Speak to me in roses.
Sing my worries to sleep.
Rock my sadness away.
Crown my heart with your
respect.
I told you.
Engulf my heart into yours.
Because a love like that
lights up
any weary sky.

My sky had been weary for
way too long
when I wrote this to you.

I miss you every time it
rains
and every time
the sun shines bright.
The rain reminds me of
the purity of your voice,
and the sun reminds me of
the beauty of your presence.

It's okay to miss you.
It only means I once loved you.

It's not you I miss.
It's who you used to be.

I fell in love with you
little by little
and in more than one place.
I left a piece of your love
in each place
forever.
I used to feel drowned in your love
every time I visited any of those
places,
and my face would turn red
because of the depth of my love for you.
Now I just feel pain.
It's not that I
want your love back.
It's just that I no longer wish to be
in places where I once felt loved
and now that love has faded into
pain.

The harder it rained,
the more I knew
that I was falling in
love
with you.
The rain of you,
the droplets of you,
were taking away the
pain
of me
and quenching the thirst of
the soul
in me.

*Now I know that no one
can
take away my pain.
My pain is my own
to make my own
nectar.*

Rain planted
you
in my heart
like rain
cleansed me from
your pain.

To you,

The tears that they
caused you
can be just tears or
rain that cleanses
the sorrows out of
your soul.
You choose.

My heart drowned in the venom of
your words
as they slithered their way into my
self-worth,
broke my faith in kindness
and tainted my innocence.
They ran through my veins
like poison
and cast the night over my soul.
But my words were stronger,
my purity screamed louder,
and the pieces of my soul
revolted.
They reclaimed the throne of
my dignity that you unlawfully
occupied.

I should have known to walk
away the first time you
blamed me for
you choosing to
break me with your words.

The day you walked into my life,
I felt like the chosen one.
How could a king like him
love a free soul like mine?
How could he love you, you fool?
The distance you'd have to run is far.
Too far.
And the soldiers of the battles
you'd have to win are gone.
Long gone.
He's championed wars,
and you're still training to fight.
He's run marathons,
and you're still learning to walk.
He's conquered cities,
and you're still learning the maps.
He's sailed oceans,
and you're still building your boat.
It must be your foolish mind crafting stories with
invisible ink
and reading between lines that don't exist.
Then you told me that you loved my smile.
And the time after that,
you asked me what perfume it was that I wore.
I felt so lucky that a man like you
wanted me in a kingdom like yours.
And when the gates opened and I entered inside,
I saw nothing that pleases the eye.
You see, you worked so hard to build your fort,
but forgot to tidy what's inside.
The years had tainted your every corner
with the torture that you'd inflicted on every visitor.
And now I look back and think
what a fool you were to think
that you could conquer a queen's kingdom like mine.
What a fool.

You waltzed your way into my life
when you knew that the entry was forbidden.
I never knew that love could be forced
into a human's heart
until you forced me to love you.
You convinced me that loving you would be
noble, because
who would love someone like you but
"a heart of gold"?
You told me that you loved how innocent my vision of
the world was,
how nonjudgmental my heart could be.
You told me that you loved my
honesty, sincerity, and kindness,
and a few more things that made blood
rush to my face.
I was a free bird.
You broke my wings and
caged me in your misery.
You asked me to stay when
you knew that you should have
let me go.
And when you decided that you
no longer needed me,
you let go of my hand.
You told me to take a step back
and give my head a shake.
You told me that I was delusional
and that your words were just words.
I used to sing melodies;
now I cry tears.
I get lost in thought sometimes,
and I wonder to myself,
if it was noble to love a man like you,
is it not disgraceful to torture
a woman like me?

Invisible Threads

The tears storming in my heart
woke me up
as the night sky rained
invisible threads
like the ones you weaved.
They asked me,
"What would you tell
your daughter if
her heart cries this way
over a man
one day?"
That is when I knew
every answer
I needed to know.

I used to write my poems for
you.
Now I write to forget
about you.

And it's sad, because
I remember you now that you're
gone
more than I remembered you
when you were
still here.

I tell the traces of
your memories,
the face that is no longer
one I wish to see,
and the love that no longer
feels like love:

Love me because
you want to,
not because I
ask you to.

One rainy day,
when it was clear to me
that you loved me,
I was too afraid
to admit that
I loved you in return.
You asked me how I was doing,
and I just told you that
I loved it when it rained.
A few moments of
beautiful silence
passed us by
where I felt your love
raining,
hailing,
into my heart.
I knew that
I was in too deep
when you said:
"It's still raining."

If I wrapped you inside my heart
to make you feel the pain
that you planted in my heart
the moment you walked away,
you would never walk away.
And I would be wrapped in your arms
right now,
not your memories.

My soul is aching to
let you go
when corners of you are
still imprinted
so vividly in my
soul.

You said you loved
scars
because they tell stories.
Look at the story that
you left
to intrigue every visitor
after you.

I miss you,
but I don't have the right
to miss you.
There is a part of you
that felt like home,
and I cannot find it
in anyone new.

You asked around
why I found it so hard
that you walked away.
Everyone before you
walked away.
And you were the first person
I truly believed would stay.
But you too
walked away.

I find myself trapped
in the corners of your
mind.
Please let me
out.

Now I know
that it was not you
who needed to release me.
It was me
who needed to release
you
and release
me.

I kept telling myself:

Letting go does not mean
that you are
giving up
or that you are
weak.
It could just mean that
you are no longer
allowing what hurts you
to control you.

Even if they
are the ones who want
you
to let go of them,
tell yourself that you are
letting them go because
you
want to.
You are not obeying
them.
You are liberating
your soul.

Your voice might feel faint now,
perhaps an echo, or even a whisper.

Your wings might feel broken now,
perhaps exhausted or
too weak to fly.

Your heart might hurt now,
perhaps too sensitive or
too fragile to feel.

Your light might seem
dim
right now,
perhaps trying to shine
when it's already light outside.

And perhaps you will not believe me when
I tell you, but
I will tell you.

Your voice will roar one day,
and they will have to listen.

Your wings will spread one day,
and they will watch you fly higher.

You will heal one day,
and you will fly over the walls that they
built in your face.

Your light will strike through
the sky one day,
for you are the sun.
And the sun rises
every day.

If you tell me that
softness
is weakness,
don't you dare tell me that
hardness
is strength.
If you tell me that
kindness
is weakness,
don't you dare
tell me that bitterness is
strength.
Sir, take your cruelty
out of my kingdom.
And allow my soft heart to
crown my mind with
the strength in my kindness.

I scream this in your face,
in my mind,
every time I remember
that time you told me that
I was too soft.

Every day, tell yourself this:

Keep your heart kind
no matter how dark the world gets.
You own only yourself.
You can only control your actions.
Keep your heart beautiful.
The world needs that.

I say it to myself,
too.

May the beauty of your heart be the
reason they love you.

Never change your heart
just to change who loves you.

A message to the one
who broke me:

I hope
from the bottom of my heart
that no one ever hurts you
the way you hurt me.
I could easily wish you pain,
but you hurt me so much
that I would never wish it
upon my enemies,
let alone someone I loved.

It's simple.
If they hurt
you,
they need help,
not
you.

To you, and
to the me who stared at the
mirror for hours
seeing someone
foreign
to the soul that disappeared from
my eyes:

I see your pain, and
I find myself wishing that
I could take it
away.
It pains me because
I understand
exactly
how you feel.
And when I was in your
shoes,
all I wanted to hear was
"I understand."
So I will tell you now:
I understand, and
it's okay that you are hurting,
because that means that
you
are
human.

I understand.

The struggle to get you out of my head:

You are the
beginning and
the end of
my every story.
Day.
And night.
Leave my endings.
I beg you.

It's a shame for you
that you chose not
to fight the wars
in my battlefield.
It's a shame for you
that you were a coward
and waved your white flag.
You surrendered.
What a shame.
The king who will own my heart
must be brave enough
to endure the chaos of purity within
me.

Now I know that
no king can
own
my heart.
I am the owner of my own
empire.

The same light that
attracted the butterfly in me
to you
is the one that wounded
my wings
and stopped me from flying.
But I got back up,
darling,
and my wings
are so much stronger
than they were before.

When you walk away from
the source
of pain,
you start healing.

Other Places

What will you say when they ask you,
"Why did you let her go?"
If it was her sadness,
that is what made her real.
If it was her sensitivity,
that is what made her considerate.
If it was her unconditional love for you,
that is what made her loyal to you.
But it's true, you know,
that we walk away from what is real
because we're too afraid
of staying in one place.
She built a home for you,
but you still had other places to see.

My future son:

When you find her,
put diamonds on her
heart
before you put them on
her ring.

If it hurts your soul,
let go of it.

You left my soul
through my
tears.
Extracting you from
inside of me
took the sadness
out of me.

If I have to tell you
how to love me
or what to tell me,
keep your love and
keep our words.
I don't want them.

Break.

Let your soul
discover
the power it has
to build a
masterpiece.

*That masterpiece
is
you.*

You are not what they
did to
you.
You are not the pain
that they caused
you.
You are
a hero who
endured
the struggle.

I salute you.

After you finally
close your door,
some will come back to knock,
just to check whether you will open
or not.
If you do,
they will pretend that they
are only
visiting to see how
you are
doing.

They really are checking if
you still care.

To my new love:

Forgive me if my
insecurities are
speaking loudly.
When you are afraid of
not being loved for
who you are,
because you have been
not loved
and told that it was because of
who you are,
your insecurities start
speaking.
I let you see my
insecurities because
I want to see you
fall in love with me
and
my insecurities.

You would think that
a wilted flower
could not possibly wilt
anymore.
Look at me,
and you will
understand.

I say this every time
my soul
feels exhausted but
the nectar in me reminds me
of the love in me.

Believe me when
I tell you that
the sadness in your soul
will leave.
And trust me when
I tell you that
you have the power
to decide when
you want it to leave.
It will be painful.
It will be a mountain.
It will be an uphill battle.
But once you finally
cleanse it out,
happiness will trickle in
like raindrops
quenching the thirst of your
soul.

Don't move the mountain.
Climb it.

You deserve the kind of love
that will make you want to be
a better person,
for you first
and then for them.
Promise me that you
will not
accept less.
Promise me that you
will not
compromise your own
inner beauty to have
anyone
"complete" you or
to have
anyone
make you feel
"worth it."
You are worth it.
No doubt.
So please.
Please.
Do not accept
less.

Tell their voices:

No.
I am not
what you say of me.
No.
I am
what I do.
Just like you are not
what I say of you.
No.
You are
what you do.

Why did you tell me
what you did not mean
and then punish me for
believing you?

Their failure to love
themselves
should not make you hate them.
They need love.
Love them.

I can't tell you that you
will not get hurt.
Just remember that light breeds light.
Spread light.
It will come back to you
one day,
some way,
somehow.

If you don't believe in
yourself,
don't *expect*
anyone to believe in
you.

Your smile makes you
beautiful.
Keep smiling.
You don't know whose
day your smile will make.

I hope that your smile
makes your day
first.

Yesterday, you chose to
leave.
And today,
I
am choosing to let
you
go.

Because
I don't want
you
in my
tomorrow.

What I choose
today
frees my soul from carrying the mountains
from my yesterday to my
tomorrow.

If you know the end,
don't start.

*Only when you know that
going back to your
source of pain
is what you want to
restart.*

They shatter your
pieces,
and then they tell you
that they cannot
love someone who's
this broken.

They forbid you to
blame them so
you start blaming
yourself.

If they cut down the tree
that you're resting on,
spread your wings and
seek another tree.
And on the way,
explore the wonder
around you.
Learn when to face
the wind
and when to
walk with it.

Your strength comes from
within you.
Don't ever allow anyone
to bully you into feeling
weak
or into feeling like
your strength
depends on their approval.
Be your own judge.
You are your own judge.

I sincerely hope that
your soul finds peace.
You broke me, but it was only
because you were broken.
I will heal because I know that
I need to,
but I worry that you will never
realize
that you are in need of
healing.

I repeat.

I hope that
your soul finds
peace
and that your heart
reaches
home.
I hope that
lights
light up your way
and that
happiness
takes over the
pains of
your yesterday.

*Set peace to the fire
in your soul.*

Today,
I decided to forgive you.
Not because you apologized
or because you acknowledged
the pain that you caused me,
but because my soul
deserves
peace.

I will not deny my soul
its rights.

It took losing
you
to find
myself.
The day that
you walked away from
me,
I started taking
footsteps
towards myself.

Thank you
for putting me at the crossroads
between
finding myself and
making you want me.
I chose me.

The places that do not
want
you
are mirrors of the corners
in your soul that are
afraid
to be alone.

Some kinds of sadness
don't leave us,
not because we want
to be sad,
but because we want
to keep reminding
our souls
of how brave they were
to overcome such
pain.

*I hope that
you have the courage
to allow peace
into your soul,
because you are peace
and peace is you.
You deserve peace, and
peace deserves
you.*

Why do you want the
love
of those who do not
love you
and then complain that
no one
loves you?
They are not
everyone
for you to say
that no one
loves you.

I hope you find a love that
builds you,
empowers you,
and strengthens you.
I hope you find a love
that makes you love
to love.

You are unique, and
that's a fact.
Your existence is in
your hands.
So let it shine.
Let it inspire.
Let it be free.

Love,
you are the sun.
Don't you let their
silence
tell you
otherwise.

I know that it's hard.
I also know that it's
temporary.
It is building
you.
Stay strong.
The storm will be over
soon.

Tell these words to
anyone struggling
before you tell them how they
should or
should not
feel.

Perhaps you loved the person
that you wanted
them to be.

And perhaps,
just perhaps,
they loved you because
you loved who
they wanted to be.

But people change.
You don't have to
understand
the reasons.

Sometimes, our need for
closure
delays the
closure.

May the pain of the hurt
that they caused
you
stop you from hurting anyone else,
because you know how
the pain
feels.

Let
pearls
drop from your words.

You are an oyster of
love,
kindness,
and truth.

Sometimes, you can't
just wait for the tables
to turn.
Sometimes, you have to
change the table that you
are sitting at.

You are bigger than
revenge.
You are bigger than
karma.
Keep your soul
pure.

Where you left me.

-Part 1-

One day, you will look back
to find me
where you left me.
You will find the chains
that you left on my heart
where you left me.
You will find the shattered pieces
of the broken promises that you made
lying on the ground
where you left me.
You will find the suffocating aches
that you caused my heart
flying in the air
where you left me.
But, no, my love,
you will not find me.
The wind will tell you that
the poison you left me with
poisoned the hatred inside of me
that I had for myself.
The poison that you left me with
poisoned my inability to forgive my soul
for suffocating my soul.
The wind will tell you that
I am free.
You planted me like a tree
where you left me.
But did you know, my love,
that I was a bird?
And birds cannot be tamed.

-Part 2-

I found my freedom
where you left me.

I spread my wings
where you left me.

So wait for me, my love.
Perhaps I will show up
in a dream,
or a wish,
or a soft breeze,
where you left me.

Cry your heart
back
together.

You are so afraid of
allowing the ocean within you
to rage through your
eyes.

Did you not know that
your soul
suffocates on the tears that you
hold in
out of the fear of
them seeing that
you are weak.

Crying is not weakness.
Crying is the resilience of your soul
in the purest form.

You don't have to wait for people
to tell you that they're walking away.
People don't always communicate through
words.
Actions speak louder than words,
remember?
If they're gone through action,
then let them go.
What good do words do
when the action
has already been done.

Your cowardice to say that you
no longer wish to stay
put my soul through
confusion and guilt
for uttering the words
that you could not say:
"I think this is the end."

I will not wait for you
to regret losing me.
Does the sun wait for
the earth to regret
turning?
Does the moon wait for
the night to regret ending?
The sun remains the sun,
and the moon remains the moon.
I will remain myself
with or without
your acknowledgment of
my value.

Back then,
I used to say that
I don't want you to regret
losing me.
I wanted you to
not lose me.
I wanted you to
stay.

You may charm them with
your smile.
You may catch their attention with
your eyes.
You may hypnotize them
with your glow.
A look from your eyes
may be their goal.
But if your heart is truly
sincere,
you will let go of all of this.
You may ask why.
Let me tell you.
One day, your smile will look a lot less
charming.
One day, your eyes will be a lot less
piercing.
One day, your glow will be colonized by
wrinkles.
Who will look at your heart then?
Definitely not those who did not see it when
your youth was at its best.
Please do not let superficial attention
fool you.
Let true love seep through
your soul,
into your heart,
past your outer shell.

*I will tell this to my daughter
one day.*

Can a heart contain two
beats at once?
Can a sun rise upon you
twice a day?
Can you take two breaths
at once?
Can your face contain
a genuine smile with a
grieving tear?
How many words can your lips
pronounce
at once?
How many roads can your feet bear
at once?
And can you for a second be in two places
at once?
Can the sun rain?
Can the clouds shine?
Can you live two lives at once?
Tell me now.
Can a heart fit two loves
at once?

Do not
ever
accept being
another love in a person's
heart.

After all of this,
I realize that you never really
knew me.
I never really knew me
either.

Don't base your self-worth
on the words of those who
don't even know the real you,
including you.

Before I fell in love,
I always knew I wanted this:

I want you to love my heart
before you love my face,
love my vision
before you love my eyes,
love my wisdom
before you love the comfort that
my thoughts give you,
love my silence
before you love my words,
love my compassion
before you love how helpful I can be,
love the person that I am
before you love the person that
I want to be.
Respect me
before you love me.
I promise you no less than that
in return.

Now I know that saying this
is not enough.
The love that you accept
is the love that you will get.

*It is not love if it
does not
make you feel
loved.*

I see sadness in your eyes,
and I don't understand it.

I don't understand why it's there,
and I don't understand why I see it.

Tell me, where did you get the strength
to build a home for sadness in
the sea of your eyes?

Did you use bricks of tears to build its walls?
Did you make a garden around it with every love
that you loved
that broke you?

Tell me, did you protect it with every hollow hope
you had?

Open the door
and let it leave.

Allow happiness to colonize this home.

I wish someone told me this
when sadness drowned my heartbeats.
So I say it to
you.

You do not
need
what does not
want
you.

You should not
want
what does not
want
you.

I beg you to keep
your soul
healthy.

When I decided to walk away
from this shadow of
what I convinced myself was love:

You don't want me to
leave,
but you will not say or
do anything
that tells me that
you want me to stay.
Only after I leave,
you choose to claim that
I
broke
your
soul.

And all the times that
I
broke my soul in front of
you,
shattering my tears through
my eyes,
telling you that
I love you
and that I need to feel
your presence
meant absolutely
nothing to you.

When preparing for them to leave:

If things between us
come to an end,
I hope I have the
courage
to say that it was just not meant to be.
I hope that my mind does not
think back to every word
you said,
because the moment you decide to
walk away
is the moment you prove
that you never meant
a word you said.
I hate lying,
and I hate hatred,
so I hope I have the courage
not to hate you,
but only hate what you did.

There is no right way to
prepare for their departure.
It is just like preparing for
someone you love
to die.
You don't want them to.
But they do.

I burned all of the
unsent
letters inside of me
for you.
I do not want your
love
if you do not come
with it.

Today,
I choose to start
something new.

I listen to the sound
of the same rain
that I listened to
the night that your love
fell into my soul.
And I cry my tears
as I feel this new rain
cleansing my soul of you.
I did not want your soul
to leave,
but I cannot
force you
to stay.

Why are you insisting on staying
in my mind?
You're the one who decided to
leave.

You left before I could even
taste the nectar
in you.

They tell me to forget about
you
because you're not
worth it.
As if I haven't
tried.
Believe me when I say
that if I could,
I would erase
you
from my life
forever,
but you are always
on my mind,
even when
I hate you.

I do not hate
you.

They told me that they saw you
knocking on my door
with roses in your hands.
You thought I'd be waiting,
but
I built myself a new home.

Thank you for
remembering me
after I forgot you.

I am glad that
I spent time with
myself long enough to
not see you again.

I attached myself
to the parts of
you
that you
yourself
were not
attached to.

Attachment detaches you
from yourself.

Stop building
castles in skies
that are not your
own.

Do not settle
for the parts of them
that no one else
wanted.

You will one day
meet someone who will
make room in their soul
for the
beautiful
pieces of
you.

May their soul be
the home
of your love,
because homes
protect,
and your love is
a pearl:
too precious.

I want your roses with
your thorns.
Roses are tender.
They will soothe my heart.
Thorns are sharp.
They will teach me how
not to use
the thorns of my own.

Choose them because
you love them,
not because you are
afraid of
being alone.

Choose them because
they are right for
you,
not because you want to be
with
someone.

It's simple,
I know,
but we often forget what we
know
in pursuit of what we
want.

Just like their love for
you
fell out of
them,
new people will come
whose love for
you
will make love fall back
into
you.

The nectar of your
pain
will attract the right
humans to you.

It is not love that
you fall
into.
It is love
that falls
into you.

Even though your eyes
speak of the
broken promises that
someone once made,
someone's eyes
somewhere
will speak of
the love that they have for your
brokenness.

All of the places that let
you
go
are leading you to
your
home.

I forgot to forget about
you
when I tried to
forget
you.

I run from you
to
you.
You are
every destination
I ever knew.

You broke my heart into
pieces.
Now that it's open,
I can see how much love
it has inside.
I can see how much love
every piece of it deserves,
and that's not the love that
you gave me.
So thank you for allowing
me to see
how much love
I have inside of me.

There is a sadness attached
to some endings that
no beginning
can ever erase.

My heart tells me every night:

Let go of the hurt.
Let go of the pain.
Stay pure,
as you've always been.
Forgive them.
Forgive yourself.
Release them.
Release yourself.
Tomorrow is a new day.
Fall asleep with nothing
in your heart but
love.

I am sensitive.
It means that when I laugh,
I laugh my heart out.
And when I cry,
the birds in the sky
cry with me.
When I see pain in your eyes,
I feel it in my heart.
My sensitivity makes me
real.
If you want me,
know that I will not
leave my sensitivity
to be loved by
anyone.

You chose to let me go.
My gift to you is
twenty years of
walking away.

When they see that you
actually moved on,
they might come back and
tell you that they are happy
that you gave them space and that
you've become in control of your
emotions.
Don't fall for that.
They only want the thrill of
having you care about them
again,
and once you do,
they will walk away.
Again.

You say that I mean
nothing
to you,
but you search for my eyes
in the face of every woman
you meet.
You search for my warmth
in the soul of every woman
you seek.
You think that
if time and circumstance
forced you to force me
out of your life,
that time and circumstance
owe you
a woman like me.
Search, my darling.
Search.

I do not come
twice
in the eternity that passed
nor in the one to come.

Your sky no longer
means a thing
to me,
for I am in a totally
different universe.

*Keep your clouds out of my
sky.*

The worst kind of
pain
is the one that you
feel but
cannot express.

Your words cause a
storm inside of you,
trying to escape through
your eyes or
your skin, but
your silence cages them
inside.

You asked me:
"How can I make the ending of
us
easier on you?"

"Stay."

In a coffee shop
one day,
you will see me sitting
next to the window,
sipping on my coffee
the same way
I used to
and looking out the window
the same way
I used to.
You will wonder if I still think about you
the same way
I used to
or if I am still waiting for you to come back
the same way
I used to.

You better walk away, because
I no longer crave you in my life
the same way I used to.

Oh, little voice of mine,
they want to weaken you.
Stay strong.
They want to silence you.
Stay alive.
They want you to follow.
Revolt.
They want you to speak to impress them.
Speak honestly.
They want to dim your grace.
Stay kind.
Oh, little voice of mine,
remember when you're heard one day
to give a voice to the
unheard.

You escaped my soul
through my tears.
My love for you was as
deep
as the ocean,
and that's how far down I dove.
I cried enough to fill the ocean
and float my soul back
to shore.

I hope one day
when the tables turn
that I am no longer
sitting at them.
I have no interest in
helping karma
take its course,
nor am I interested in treating
them
the way they treated
me.

We run from attachment to
attachment,
as if that is the solution.
The problem is that
we fail to love
ourselves
without someone loving
us.
And we fail to see
our self-worth
without someone seeing
it.

*Do not detach from yourself
to attach to someone else.*

When new love comes along:

I am so afraid of
giving you the pieces of
my soul that
I gave before.

They are still hurting and
perhaps too
fragile
to trust again.

When new love comes along,
it might feel like this:

Your kind of love
makes me want to love
again.

It makes me want to
forget about every love
that turned out to be
not love

and fly into the ocean of
you
and dip into the sky of
you.

You left, too.
But thank you for allowing me to
write about love
again.

If your sky is
a lot clearer without
me,
I will not be a cloud
in your space.
May the love that
finds you
put sunshine in your sky.
I will work on cherishing
the clouds in my soul
that cause rainbows
after the rain.

Leave me to my sadness if
you do
not
understand it.
Don't pretend to
care
if you don't.
Don't pretend to know the
way.
Because you don't.

No one does.

Why do you love feeling
when you fall in love but
hate it when you're in
pain?
How do you expect pain to leave you if
you
do not
feel it
so it can leave
you?

Let it hurt you.
Let it drain you.
Let it destroy you.

For only after your destruction will you
rebuild an extraordinary masterpiece of
your soul and say:
"I own all that I am."

So go ahead. Crumble.

Just because they
deny
that they caused you
pain,
it does not mean that they
didn't.

Why do you still believe them
anyway?

If you have to beg for
their love, then
it's not love.

Giving love because you
feel it
is different from giving it because
you have to.

To the one who comes into my life:

I don't want the stars.

I want you to capture them in my eyes as you look my way.

I don't want the moon.

I want you to capture its light and guide our way
through the darkest of nights
as you hold my hand.

I don't want the sun.

I want you to use its beautiful rays to put color into
the memories that we make together.

I don't want empty words.

I would rather meaningful silence.

I don't want things.

I want happiness.

I knew that I started
healing
when I started seeing a
future
beyond you.

When new love knocked on my door.

- Part 1-

I dove into the ocean
before I knew how to swim.

I aimed for the sun
before I had my wings.

I built castles in the sky
and forgot to build the stairs.

I claimed a crown,
but there was no kingdom in the land.

And when it all came crumbling down,
I abandoned my oceans.
I abandoned the skies.
I vowed off building castles.
I vowed off having dreams.

I vowed off jumping
because I've fallen before.
I vowed off venturing without knowing
where my destination was.

I vowed off feeling.
I vowed off love.

- Part 2-

And out of nowhere, you just came,
asking me where I came from and
what was my name.

I can tell that you're honest.
I can tell that you're genuine.

Your values and principles are
everything I've ever wished for.

But where did you come from,
asking me to trust again?

Where did you come from,
asking me to start all over again?

Where did you come from,
asking me to smile again?

Where did you come from,
asking me to love again?

I am still
bleeding from my
first wound.

Tragedy

Don't think that your
departure carving a scar
into my soul
was the tragedy.

The tragedy of someone
leaving
has been the definition of
my life.

The true tragedy is that
you had the chance to be
different and
stay.

You are no different from
anyone who came before you.

If you wanted to be different,
you should have stayed.

To choose to fall in love is
to choose to take
a risk.

To be hurt or
let go is
a tragedy.
And it is
possible.

But to choose to
not
take the risk and
miss the chance of finding the love of
your life is
a bigger tragedy.

And it is also possible.

I stopped choosing you
months after
you stopped choosing
me.
You let me go so easily because
you never really cared about me.
And if you did,
I was not worth the fight.
I could not let you go because
I loved you more than anything.
You lost my love, and
I lost your
nothing.

Congratulations on losing
a love like mine.

You had my wings chained to the
ground.
And when you let
me
go,
I struggled to
fly
on my own.
You were my home.
I did not want to leave.
But now, the higher
I fly,
the smaller you become
in my eyes.

*Perhaps you could not
contain me because
you knew I was a bird
and that I would leave
one day.*

They minimize your pain by
telling you that you have
no right
to feel a certain way.
As if they are the ones breathing for
you,
living for
you,
feeling for
you.
They don't know that feeling takes
courage
and healing takes
time.
But you know that, so
have the courage and
feel.
Give yourself time to
heal.

Don't tell me how to
feel if
you don't know what it feels like to
feel the way I'm
feeling.

You add to the beauty of this world just by
being you.

Even by your imperfections and
your flaws,
by your up and
down times,
by your stresses and
your fears.
All that is different is
unique.
All that is unique is
beautiful.
Your soul is
beautiful because
it's unique.

I used to think that
you accepting me into your world
would make me
the luckiest person on earth,
as if luck belongs in
places or
humans.
Today, I
am thankful that there was no place
for me
in your world.
I have created a world of my
own.
And for that,
I am lucky.

Take your empty words and
swallow them.
Take your broken promises and
untell them.
I thought you were great.
I thought you were different.
I thought you were faithful.
I thought losing you would be tragic.
I refused to see you through the eyes of
those who love me.
And I refused to see myself through
anyone's eyes but
yours.

The eyes that lied and made mine
cry
don't mean a thing to me even if I
try.

So take my heavy words and digest them.
Because you forced yours down my throat
way too many times.

Turn around and
walk away like you did before.
Don't look back, because
all you will see is
a closed
door.

Maps

All of the roads that lead to
you, I
have kept on my
map to
remind myself of
all of the places that
I should never again
head to.

My Address

Find me where
kindness
is. I
dwell in
the peace of
heart
that kindness
is.

If you ever get the chance
to treat them the way they
treated you,
no matter how hurtful it was,
I hope that you
choose
to walk away
and do better.

One day,
someone will ignore them
the way they ignored you.
One day,
someone will belittle them
the way they belittled you.
One day,
someone's voice will be
higher than theirs,
as theirs was higher than yours.
One day,
they will be defeated by someone
as they defeated you.
I just hope that someone is not
you.
You are better than treating people
the way they treat you.

If pain built a home in
your heart,
remember that it has
doors.
And it has
windows.
Open the windows to
allow happiness in.
Better yet, open the doors and
walk outside.

Happiness is at your door,
desperately waiting for you to
open the door and
let it in.
Trust your heart and
open that door.

Darling,
When did your heart become so weak?
When did the glare in your eyes fade?
When did you disappear into the darkness?
When did you start believing that you are
nothing?
Did you forget the beauty that
once shined from your soul?
Did you forget to see yourself
through your eyes before you saw yourself
through theirs?
Did you forget that happiness comes from within
you?
Smile, darling.
You are beautiful.
You don't need them to look at you
before you look at yourself.
You don't need them to love you
before you love yourself.

You are worthy of respect
no matter what their mood is.
Do not accept less.

*Your love for them speaks of
you,
not them.
Don't you ever
regret your ability to
love.*

If they know that you deserve better,
they will pretend not to want you.
They know that you will figure that out
one day.
They reject you to avoid the pain of
you leaving them.

You do not need the permission of
the one who hurt you to
feel the pain that they caused
you.
Just because they don't acknowledge it,
it doesn't mean that
it doesn't exist.

Crystal Ball

You told me to wait for you to
find yourself, so
I waited because
your love was worth it.
I lost myself waiting for
you, hoping that you
would find me with you.
And when you found yourself,
you did not find me with you.
I learned the hard way to
never put myself under the mercy of
anyone's
crystal ball.
If I cannot be in their present,
I do not want to be in their
future.

A crystal ball does not
contain you or
your glory.

When pain knocks on your door:

The pain is just meant
to cleanse you.
If I had to choose between
numbness and pain,
I'd choose to be
in pain
for years than to
put on a mask of strength
where my laugh is
empty and
my tears are too proud to spill
an ocean.
One day, the pain will end,
and
I will laugh my heart out.
It may take years, but at least
I will keep my heart
alive and pure
instead of
numb and tainted by pain that I refused
to feel.

I trusted you to not
break me further,
but you did.

You promised that you
would take care of
the pieces of me
that I trusted your heart with.
Now I know that
no one owns my pieces
if I do not own them.

To a narcissist I once loved:

I know that you are waiting
for me to break down and
contact you.
I know that you must be thinking
that I am miserable waiting for you
to give me attention.
But, you see,
I am not the person I once was.
You destroyed me over and over,
but I built myself back up
into someone you will
never
have the honor of
getting to know.

Sometimes,
the best thing you can do
for someone you love
is let them go.
Set them free.
Wish them happiness and
set them free.

Set yourself free.

Just because you are feeling
lost,
it does not mean that
you need to go back their way
even if they were the only home
you've ever known.
You left it for a reason.
Remember?
It is better to stay lost
and search for a better home
than to return to
the home that was never really
a home.

*Build your own
home.*

If your heart hurts,
be thankful.
At least you have a heart and
at least it feels.
So many out there are
in denial.
They inflict pain on others and
don't feel it.
They commit selfish acts and
call it self-love.
They break your back and tell you that
it's your fault for being in the way.
If your heart hurts,
be thankful.
At least you know that
you will not inflict pain on others because
you know how it feels.
You know that you will not love yourself if
it means hurting someone else.
You know that you will not break
someone else's back just
to get to your destination.
If your heart hurts,
love it back to peace.

Stop dwelling in the past.
No, you could not have known
better.
No, you would not do things differently
if you went back.
No, they would not have
treated you differently if
you had acted,
looked, or
cared differently.
They are who they are regardless of
who you are.
They were thrown your way
for a reason.
Accept that
you
cannot change people unless
they
want to change.
And it's not your job to
fix what's been broken by
someone else.

Just like you made the choice to
hold on,
you can make the choice to
let go.
And if it's hard, then
it must mean that you held on too tightly.
Be proud of your sincerity with your
feelings, but
realize that if holding on is
hurting you, then
you must
let
go.

I stopped choosing you when
I chose to
stop
choosing you.

One day,
the tables will turn,
and your voice will be
stronger than theirs.

One day,
you will be heard,
and they will have to listen.

One day,
you will have the opportunity
to say what you've been waiting to say.

And I hope, on that day,
that you are wise enough
to say only what needs to be said.

And walk away.

Just because they do not
listen,
it does not mean that you
are not worthy of being
heard.

Your voice may scare them because
it causes thunder
in their soul.

You are not too much of
anything.
Maybe you are too much
love,
too much
care, or
too much
innocence.
But that, there can never be
too much of.
In fact, the world is
suffering
from people who have
too little of that.

He was the best thing that
never happened to you.
And you will one day be
a choking tear
in his heart
that he is too proud to
admit
was the best thing that could have
ever
happened to him.

My heart tells me what
I don't want to hear.
That is why I listen to it.
What we want to hear
is always safe
and comfortable.
It is not always the truth.
So I've learned to listen
to what makes me uncomfortable
because I would rather
listen
to the truth by my own will
than be forced to believe it
after it hurts me.

You were not addicted to their
love.
You were addicted to their
pain.
And when their pain
left,
their love for you
left.

If their love for you
depends on what you
offer them,
it's not love.
It's abuse.
You deserve to be loved
for who you are,
even when you are
unable to give.

Be kind, because that is
who you are.
Do not allow the ignorance of
others to make you
like them.

They are not you.

So one person let you go.
One place let you go.
One idea let you go.
One dream gave up on you.
What about all the other people?
All the other places?
All the other ideas and dreams?
Are they not worth the chances that
you took
once
before?

I always imagined that
falling in love would
touch my soul before my body.
I always imagined that it would
value the beauty
inside of me before
the color of my eyes,
the fairness of my skin,
or the lipstick I chose to wear.
I always imagined that love would free me, not
enslave me.
Love to me is
pure. It is
elevating. It is
empowering. So if you don't
have that kind of love for me, then
walk away.

*I will not settle for less than what
my soul is worth.*

Unrequited Love

If I love you,
I will tell you that I love you.
And if you choose to leave,
I might beg you to stay
because
I love you.
But I cannot make you stay
if you choose to walk away.
Rest assured,
I will not pretend not to care
just to deny that you were the one to leave.
I'd rather love you and not be loved
in return by you,
and crumble in my pain over
the loss of love with you,
than pretend that my love for you
was a lie.
My strength does not come from
my pride.
It comes from my vulnerability
to break my heart open
when it is broken.

I don't miss
you.
I miss
the person I thought you were.
I did not love
you.
I loved
the person you pretended to be.

When I feel lost,
I doubt every feeling
I ever felt.

If their love one day
turns out to be
just words,
don't doubt for
a moment that you
should walk away.
And these are not
just words.

When I reminded you of
things you used to say,
you said:
"Just words."

Maybe you will live with the regret
of allowing yourself to allow
someone to put you down
and use you.
But they will one day live
with the regret
of putting someone down and
using them.
Maybe you will live with the
pain
of their words.
And maybe you will live with the
pain
of seeing them move on and go places.
But they will one day live with
the regret of using the wrong words
with you.
And they will move on to hurt
the next person.
The places they will go are nothing
because they are empty of emotion.
Their places may be grand, but
their lives are small,
so small.
You are bigger than their pain.
You are bigger than their words.
You are bigger than worrying about
where they are.
Look at your own path.

Forgive me for writing so negatively
about you.
You have love within you.
You just haven't chosen to
awaken it
yet.

You took me out of your
sky.

So I took you out of my
universe.

I feel free.

Drown me in darkness
so that I may
rise lightly
in light.

Love the hatred out of them.

If you hate them for
the hatred that they have for
you,
how will you teach them
what love truly is?

With tears in my eyes one night,
I told the stars
about you.
They listened to me as if
they had known you for
years.
They told me that I was not
the first one who had spoken to them
of your pain.
They told me to let you go, because
you had so much more pain to inflict
upon me, as you had on
others.
I listened to them and
let you go.
And a wish upon a shooting star sent me
the person I always wished for.

Me.

It hurts when
the one who broke your wings is
the one with the electric wire.
Every time you
heal a little and try to
fly again, they
break you even harder.
And every time you
try to speak, they
break your soul again
even harder.

Your soul is a bird, love.
Take a few steps away from
the pain and
fly away.

To the one who broke me,
and I hope you read this
one day:

Break,
break,
break me as much as you want.
Crack my heart
as many times as it takes
for your ego to
feel as strong as you want it to be.
That is all you will ever be;
a soul who chose to break
instead of heal.
Time has destined for you
to have power over me,
but time will turn around,
as karma does,
and I will one day have the power to
chain you,
belittle you
and use you
as you used me.
I will have that power
and instead of using it,
I will leave you
and instead of shattering your ego
some more,
I will sew it back together.
You see,
when my parents raised me,
they cautioned me of men like you.
I will not dishonor them
by wasting my heart on hurting
a nothing
like you.

I know that you want to
see them hurt
the way they hurt you.
But, believe me,
you are above that.
For them to hurt you,
they must have
pain
inside of them.
They don't need to be hurt.
They need to be healed.
I am not telling you that
it's fair for them to get
away with hurting you.
Just be the bigger,
wiser,
more understanding
person.
Don't let them make you
like them.
Wish them healing.
Wish them love.
And walk away.
Even if they chose to walk away
first.
They need to find their way.
You causing them pain
only makes you worse
and them worse.
If you can't do good for this
world,
then stand still.
But you know that
you are
better than that.

You told me what you
did not mean and then
punished me for
believing it.
And when I told you that
it was unfair, you
told me that life
is unfair.
People like you blame
anyone but themselves for
the choices
that they choose to make.
If it's not life,
it's a person, and
if it's not a person,
it's life. But
never you.

If you want to occupy a place
in my heart,
step one is to
be honest
with me.
Otherwise, turn the other way.
I only build homes in
my heart for
sincere humans.

Why are you
so quiet?
The ocean within
you
is raging.
Let your words
flow.
Let your soul
scream
gently,
kindly,
softly.

There is a part of you
that is so ready for this change.
You know it.
Just go ahead.
Wonder is
awaiting
you.
Take the risk.

It is not their true
colors that you suddenly
see.
Their colors were always
there.
It is your eyes that
colored them
with kindness.

Yet their silence
somehow
convinces you that
something is wrong with
you.

You will always be
my saddest goodbye.
And the most heartbreaking
story I will ever tell.
You will always be
the hardest lesson I had
to learn
when I did not want to
and
the reason I learned
to never
put someone before me.
You will always be
the best thing that
never
happened to me.
Thank you for walking away.
If you had not let go of me,
I would not have
what I have
today.

I would not be
who I am
today.

If they already broke you,
why are you still broken while
they are already breaking someone
else?

*Start building your own
empire.*

Sometimes,
a stranger can
look into your eyes
once
and not only see,
but fully understand
your sadness.
No words.
No conversations.
You just both know.
You just both get it.
And you wonder how it took
moments for a stranger
to see what those around you,
for years,
did not see.

Our eyes reflect the scars
carved into our souls.

It is not their love that you need.
It is your love for yourself that
you need.

I will repeat this as many times
as it takes
for you
to
believe it.

I was not ready for you to
let me go. You
were not ready for someone to
hold on to
you. I
hated you for giving up on me.
And you hated me for reminding you that
you are so scared of love. I
consider myself the hero for
taking a risk on you and
you the coward for
awakening someone's heart with
no intention of continuing the
journey.
I salute you.

Sarcasm has always irritated me, but
your tone must have
tainted my ability to
weigh my words properly.

To the man who once said he
loved me:

I did not ask you to
pretend
to understand me.
I did not ask you to
say that you would stay.
I did not ask you
to ask
me
to love
you.
But you did.
And I thought you understood me.
I thought you'd stay.
I thought your love would last.
But my soul became too heavy on you.
You walked away.
You left me wondering
why you chose someone broken
like me
to break even
more.

Even if you say you never intended
it,
I am still broken.

We all know that if it's not meant to be,
it will not happen.
If it's meant to be,
it will.
We all know that everything
happens for a reason.
And one day, we will know that reason.
What we need is strength
in the moment
to think that way.
It should not be easy
to not get what you want to get.
It should not be easy
to not be loved back.
It should not be easy
to work hard and not reach your destination.
It's okay to feel pain.
It takes time to accept realities
that we don't want to accept.
And just because reality is painful,
it does not mean that you are not
worthy of good things coming your way.
It means that you
must change the direction
that you are looking in.

I always wished that you
gave me a chance to show you
what life with me
would be like.
Now that I see what life
without you is like,
I understand why fate
never answered my wish.
You see, fate took care of me, and
you helped it by
causing the pain that you
caused me.

Thank you.

Forgive them
not because they asked for your
forgiveness
or because they deserve it
or because the pain they caused you
is not worth it,
but because you cannot truly
move on
without forgiving.
It shows your level of maturity and
your ability to
understand that life is not always fair
and that someone's behavior
speaks of them,
not you.
Your forgiveness speaks of you,
not them.

I thought that I needed your apology to
move on.
I really needed to forgive myself
first.

When I no longer want to be
heard by you,
that is when you will
want to listen to what
I have to say.

*It will be too late
then.*

I knew that my wanting for you
ended
when I saw you
for the first time
months later
and all I wanted to do
was vomit
nectar all over you,
to soak you,
drown you
and consume you.
I wanted to punch your face,
which I vaguely recalled,
with
kindness
and rip your heart
out of your ego and
put it back
where it belongs.

My dear reader,

I see that your heart is
heavy and
that you are struggling to carry it
and find a home.
I want to tell you that
if you ever need my help,
I will help you carry it
through my words.
I will help you find a
home.
My heart is here to
help lift yours.

My dear self,
I apologize.
For not putting you first. For
putting them first.
For making your worth dependant on how
they
saw
you.
For making their words more important than
yours. For not allowing myself to forgive you or
to forgive me.

Forgive me.

For believing them when they said that
something was wrong with you.
Forgive me for not believing in
you.
Forgive me for loving them more than
loving you.
Forgive me for
not loving you.

My heart cries every time I read this.

Stay kind.
It makes you beautiful.

Your kindness might cause you
to lose some people.
Stay kind, though.
If you lose them
because you are kind
and nice,
it's their loss,
not yours.

If you don't like my truth,
don't try to put me down,
because I will not change myself
to please you.
Just as I respect you as you are,
respect me as I am.

If your heart is kind,
your soul is golden.

Don't ever change.

In your little world,
you may be unwanted.
If you dare to look outside,
and I hope you do,
you will see that
there is a whole new world
right outside of
the cage that
you
are caging yourself
in
that loves your wings
and loves to see you
fly.

Sad Rebellion

You walk hiding
half of yourself
and a little more than half.
You don't tell them what
keeps you up at night,
nor do you tell them
what keeps you going.
You don't tell them
the things you know
you need to say.
You don't tell them what
scares you to death.
You don't tell them
what hurts you,
nor do you tell them that you care.
And somehow
in that beautiful silence,
there is a strong but
sad rebellion
against allowing love
in.

One day,
they will regret the time
they spent away from those
who love them
to stay with those
whose love they want.

If you believed in them so much,
imagine how much you can believe
in yourself.
It's magical what belief can do.
So go ahead.
Start the magic.

You know the kind of sadness that
makes you want to be
quiet?
That makes you want to be
alone?
Isolated?
Far, far away?
That makes you want to re-evaluate
everything in life?
That's not sadness.
It's an awakening within you.
Don't ignore it.
Let it overtake you so you,
yes you,
may overtake it.

Here is a hard truth
to accept:
You cannot make someone
love you.

Here is a harder truth
to accept:
The best decision that you
will ever make
is to stop wanting the love
of someone who
does not
love you.

Sadly ever after
happens too,
when we find it so hard to
let go of what we invested
so
much
time
in.

I would rather let go of years
of investing in the wrong person
and be in pain
than continue to choose
sadness.

You wonder why people always leave.
I will tell you why.
You always want to change yourself
into what they like because
you are so afraid that they
might not love you
for who you are.
You are afraid to say no
because you are afraid of
displeasing them.
You give them excuses because
that's what good people do.
They walk away because they don't
understand that it is out of love,
not weakness,
that you are like that.

Life is not fair,
but
we can choose to be
fair humans
even if life
or other humans
choose to be
unfair
to us.

I told you this when
I asked you
how you changed without
allowing me to grieve.
Your answer was:
"Life is unfair."

Let your soul flow through
these words
as you turn your pain
into nectar.
Never allow
someone's sting to make you
bitter.
Keep your kindness
kind.
Keep your love
loving.
Keep your forgiveness
forgiving.
And keep your purity
pure.

Say:
If you are disrespectful with me,
I will move out of your way, but
I will not disrespect you.
I will not be unkind to you.
I will not mirror your actions.
Who are you to make me step down
to a level
where I don't belong?

If you write about love,
they might say that you're in love.
And if you write about heartache,
they might say that you're heartbroken.
If you write about happiness,
they might wonder why you're so happy.
And if you write about sadness,
they might pretend like they didn't hear it.
If you write about loss,
they might pity you.
And if you speak the truth,
they might criticize you.
So let it be that you're in love.
Have they not been?
Let it be that you've been heartbroken.
Who is not?
Let it be that you're happy or sad.
Is it not normal?
Let it be that you've lost.
We've all lost.
But don't you ever let
what people think stop you from
expressing yourself.

Let your soul shine
through your words.

I always know how to start but
never know how to end.
I am learning to let go of
what I cannot control.
I am learning to be okay with
stories that end
in the middle.
I am learning that there is no
right way
to end.
I said it before and I will say it
again,
there is a sadness attached to endings
that no beginning can erase.

Stories that mean
something
to us
never end when or how
we want them to.
But for new stories to begin,
old ones must end.

If they love you,
they won't change you.
If they love you,
they won't break your wings.
They won't cage you
or stop you from flying.
If they love you,
they will actually
love
you.

Love tastes of sweetness,
nectar,
and
respect.

Someone,
somewhere,
is looking for the exact same love
that you have to offer.
The exact same love that
the one who hurt you did not appreciate.
Don't lose hope.
And don't settle.
The most beautiful love stories are those that
come after you realize what you deserve
and you actually finally get it.
You deserve someone who loves your
way of love.
Someone who loves you.

Because you are a good heart

Here's the thing about people with good hearts. They give you excuses when you don't explain yourself. They accept apologies you don't give. They see the best in you when you don't need them to. At your worst, they lift you up, even if it means putting their priorities aside. The word "busy" does not exist in their dictionary. They make time, even when you don't. And you wonder why they're the most sensitive people. You wonder why they're the most caring people. You wonder why they are willing to give so much of themselves with no expectation in return. You wonder why their existence is not so essential to your well-being. It's because they don't make you work hard for the attention they give you. They accept the love they think they've earned, and you accept the love you think you're entitled to. Let me tell you something. Fear the day when a good heart gives up on you. Our skies don't become gray out of nowhere. Our sunshine does not allow the darkness to take over for no reason. A heart does not turn cold unless it's been treated with coldness for a while.

To you, dear reader:

I hope that you found
yourself
in one of my pages.
I have stories within me that
novels
cannot contain.
I am afraid that I will
die
before I give birth to the words
in my soul
through my lips.
Thank you
for walking this
journey
with my soul.
I sincerely hope that
you now have the courage
to climb over
the mountains
in your way.

Love,
Najwa

Made in the USA
Middletown, DE
05 June 2017